How to survive and succeed as a SENCo *in the primary school*

Veronica Birkett

Acknowledgements

Veronica Birkett would like to thank John Eden for his belief that one day this book would be completed and published; Beth Evans, aged 6, for her contributions; and her neighbours in the adjoining semi for their ability to live a quiet life, and consequently allow her the peace she needed to get on with writing this book. Finally, she thanks the many SENCos she has been privileged to meet and from whom she has learned so much.

Extracts on pages 11, 19 and 21 were reproduced by permission of the publisher, Vermilion, from *Chicken Soup for the Soul*, 1993.

For extra copies of this book please call Customer Services on 01945 463441.

Permission to Photocopy
This book contains worksheets which may be reproduced by photocopier or other means for use by the purchaser. This permission is granted on the understanding that these copies will be used within the educational establishment of the purchaser. This book and all its contents remain copyright. Copies may be made without reference to the publisher or the licensing scheme for the making of photocopies operated by the Publishers' Licensing Agency.

How to survive and succeed as a SENCo in the primary school
LL01236
ISBN 1 85503 311 9
© Veronica Birkett
Illustrated by Rebecca Barnes
All rights reserved
First published 2000
Revised 2002
LDA, Duke Street, Wisbech, Cambs PE13 2AE
3195 Wilson Drive, Grand Rapids, MI 49544, USA

Contents

Contents

Setting
the scene

Introduction
Setting the scene

Who will benefit
from this book?

Who will benefit from this book?

This book has been written for, and is dedicated to, Special Educational Needs Co-ordinators (SENCos), to assist them in their difficult and demanding role. It takes account of the Special Educational Needs Code of Practice, issued in November 2001, which took effect in January 2002.

The role of the SENCo

The role of the SENCo

What exactly does the role of SENCo entail?

According to the 2002 Code of Practice, the following points define what is expected from a SENCo in a mainstream primary school. A SENCo is responsible for:

- overseeing the day-to-day operation of the school's special educational needs (SEN) policy;
- liaising with and advising fellow teachers;
- managing the learning support assistants (LSAs);
- co-ordinating provision for children with SEN;
- overseeing the records of all pupils with SEN;
- liaising with parents of children with SEN;
- contributing to the in-service training of staff;
- liaising with external agencies, including the educational psychology service and other support agencies, medical and social services and voluntary bodies.

What does all this mean when translated into reality?

The reality: the role of SENCo is – challenging!

It is rare to discover a SENCo who is just that. Usually a juggling act between being a full-time class teacher and carrying out the role is involved. Early-morning or after-school review meetings are common and the hours of administration and paperwork involved often mean additional weekend work for already busy teachers. Other onerous tasks may include persuading class teachers to carry out the recommendations on Individual Education Plans (IEPs) and dealing with possible confrontations with distressed, bewildered or even irate parents who are concerned about their child's special need. Finding sufficient time to meet all the demands of the job may be difficult and frustrations may occur when some pupils appear to be making very little progress towards meeting their learning targets. Parents may not turn up to review meetings; the LSA may be finding it difficult to work with their allocated pupil. The room designated for the meeting with the educational psychologist is suddenly occupied by a class. The SENCo weekly release time is temporarily lost because ... The list of possible grievances is endless. Why on earth would anyone want to take on the role in the first place?

The benefits of taking on the role of SENCo are – plentiful!

Perhaps it's the personal satisfaction of knowing that at last a particular pupil is making progress, that targets have been achieved, that parents are feeling encouraged and taking more interest, and that the child is growing in confidence. In addition, SENCos may experience the gratitude of a class teacher who was despairing until the SENCo's intervention. The teacher responsible for the role will often attract the respect and support of the head and governors who will, of course, be aware of how an effective special needs department impacts on the general standards achieved by the school.

The positive aspects of the role also extend to a personal level, as SENCos will have opportunities to develop their own skills and knowledge. They will meet many different professionals and be able to learn from them. They will have opportunities to forge closer links with parents and acquire a greater understanding of how family dynamics can affect their pupils. The SENCo will learn how to analyse difficulties faced by pupils and which strategies and resources are effective. Management skills will be learned, and opportunities to develop skills as a trainer and INSET provider come with the job. But most of all, SENCos will have the satisfaction of knowing that they are carrying out a worthwhile job which may have long-term effects on pupils who, without their support and guidance, may struggle throughout their school careers.

Of course, in order to reap these undoubted benefits, SENCos need to be effective, hence this book. I hope the guidance offered will help SENCos gain greater job satisfaction and provide them with clear ideas regarding the management, structure and systems of the department. The ideas and suggestions here are not handed down from an ivory tower, but have been tried and tested in real schools, with real SENCos, and are guaranteed to enhance the efficiency of the SENCo and relieve some of the stress. This should ensure not only survival, but success and satisfaction as well.

Food for thought

100 years from now it will not matter what my bank account is, what sort of house I live in, what kind of car I drive, but the world may be a different place because I was important in the life of a child.

Successories

'I wandered lonely as a cloud ...'

'I wandered lonely as a cloud ...' Advice: don't!

The SENCo cannot stand alone, and success will depend on the delegation of responsibility for special needs provision within the school to all those involved (more about this in Section One). Other crucial factors which impinge on the role include the amount of time allocated for the SENCo to meet administrative demands and attend meetings, the amount of training received, and the amount of funding allocated for special needs pupils. These and other issues cannot be addressed in this book, but it may be useful for you to fill in the questionnaire on page 8 to provide you, as SENCo, with an overview of your existing situation and what your overall needs are. Below is an example of a completed questionnaire to give you some ideas. If you find there are issues that need to be addressed, examine your completed questionnaire and prepare an action plan to tackle problems and identify what your future needs will be. Your head will then at least be aware that there are things that are preventing you from carrying out the role as efficiently as you would wish. All too often, when the SENCo has finally gone off with nervous exhaustion or resigned from the job, heads have been heard to say that they were not even aware that there was a problem! Identify difficulties, visit your head and see what happens.

Food for thought!

It would be useful for you to fill in this questionnaire prior to reading the book. It will be even more useful if, on completion, you are able to clarify what your needs are and design an action plan as a way forward.

Define what you mean by carrying out the role of SENCo successfully.
① All pupils identified and on the SE.
② All pupils who need them have appropriate individual Education Plans, which are reviewed / monitored regularly.
③ All paperwork in place and up to date. ④ Well established administrative systems ⑤ All staff clear about their roles --- * (I have run out of space!)

Yes [ ] No [✓] In your particular situation, would you say that your implementation of the role is completely successful?

If not, would you say it is for any of the following reasons:

Yes [ ] No [✓] Have you received adequate training to enable you to carry out the role effectively?
I am a new SENCO. The only training I have received was from the previous SENCO. (one hour)

Yes [✓] No [ ] Does the role of SENCo lack status within the structure of your school?
I find it difficult to persuade staff to fill in paperwork - always have to ask for it.

Yes [✓] No [ ] Is sufficient time allocated for you to carry out the role of SENCo efficiently and effectively?
One day per week. Seems fine, but do I make the best use of it?

Yes [ ] No [✓] Does a lack of resources to address the problems of pupils with special needs contribute to lack of success?
School has lots of SEN resources. Not used much though.

Yes [ ] No [✓] Are there sufficient learning support assistants employed to support pupils with special needs?
The only pupils with LSA support are those with statements.

Yes [ ] No [✓] Have teachers and support staff received adequate training in dealing with pupils with special educational needs?
Don't feel confident enough to provide it!

Yes [✓] No [ ] Are there any other reasons that you feel contribute to the lack of success of your particular situation? If yes, note them here.
Main reason is my lack of training. Also, would like to meet with other SENCos to see what they do. Staff and LSAs need more training too.

Information for an Action Plan

It would be useful for you to fill in this questionnaire prior to reading the book. It will be even more useful if, on completion, you are able to clarify what your needs are and design an action plan as a way forward.

Define what you mean
by carrying out the
role of SENCo
successfully.

Yes No

In your particular situation, would you say that your implementation of the role is completely successful?

If not, would you say it is for any of the following reasons:

Yes No

Have you received adequate training to enable you to carry out the role effectively?

Yes No

Does the role of SENCo lack status within the structure of your school?

Yes No

Is sufficient time allocated for you to carry out the role of SENCo efficiently and effectively?

Yes No

Does a lack of resources to address the problems of pupils with special needs contribute to lack of success?

Yes No

Are there sufficient learning support assistants employed to support pupils with special needs?

Yes No

Have teachers and support staff received adequate training in dealing with pupils with special educational needs?

Yes No

Are there any other reasons that you feel contribute to the lack of success of your particular situation? If yes, note them here.

It is important for you to have the support of other SENCos. If you are fortunate enough to be part of a cluster group of SENCos from neighbouring primary schools who meet regularly to discuss topical issues or buy in the services of a trainer, all well and good. These cluster groups may sometimes share the costs of useful resources such as test materials which are not used often, making them available to a number of schools. It is also a good idea to communicate with other SENCos through the SENCo Forum, which is co-ordinated by the British Educational and Technology Communications Agency (BECTA). It can be found at www.becta.org.uk/senco/sources/senfor.

Now it is time to read on. I hope you enjoy reading this book and that you are able to gain some ideas that will reduce your workload and allow you more free time for other things – like the rest of your life.

What is this life if, full of care,
We have no time to stand and stare?
W.H. Davies

What is this life if, full of care,

We have no time to stand and stare?

W.H. Davies

Section One
Special educational needs: identification, roles and responsibilities

Who should be identified, when and how?

It is very important for all those involved with provision for special needs to be aware of the implications and responsibilities of their role. The SENCo cannot stand alone, and as SENCo your first task may be to ensure that all members of staff are fully aware of the SEN policy of the school and just what is expected of them. In this section we shall seek to clarify the roles of the class teacher, the SENCo, the parent and the pupils themselves.

Early identification

The Code of Practice (COP) emphasises the need to identify pupils at the earliest possible time (COP page 46 paragraph 5.11). There can be no doubt of the wisdom of this statement. However, the 2002 SEN Code emphasises the need for teachers to support less able pupils within the classroom, ensuring that most of them will not be identified as having a special educational need requiring additional provision. The Code says (page 63, paragraph 6.18); 'Effective management, school ethos and the learning environment, curricular, disciplinary and pastoral arrangements can help some special educational needs arising … schools should not assume that pupils' learning difficulties always result solely, or even mainly, from problems within the young person, Pupils' rates of progress can sometimes depend on how well or what they are taught.' Teachers should give consideration to the following areas.

- **Is differentiation adequate for all pupils in all subjects?**

- **Are learning support assistants skilfully deployed in the support of low achieving pupils?**

- **Are resources adequate to meet the needs of all pupils within the classroom environment?**

- **Are issues regarding the low self-esteem, often experienced by low achievers, taken into account?**

- **Are the individual learning styles of pupils taken into account and a multi-sensory approach adopted by teachers?**

I – am – in – the – slow
read – ers – group – that – is
all – I – am – in – I
hate – it.

from 'Slow Reader'
by Allan Ahlberg

Mother to Son

Well, son, I'll tell you:
Life for me ain't been no
    crystal stair.
It's had tacks in it.
And splinters,
And boards torn up,
And places with no carpet
    on the floor —
Bare.
But all the time
I'se been a-climbin' on,
And reachin' landin's
And turnin' corners,
And sometimes goin' in
    the dark
Where there ain't been
    no light.
So, boy, don't you turn back,
Don't you set down on
    the steps
'Cause you finds it's kinder
    hard.
Don't you fall now—
For I'se still goin', honey,
I'se still climbin'
And life for me ain't been
    no crystal stair.

Langston Hughes

○ **Are teachers able to identify the particular area of special need experienced by individual pupils?**

○ **Are teachers aware of what outside help is available to them before a pupil is identified as having a special educational need?**

○ **Are parents sufficiently involved and informed of their children's progress?**

○ **Does planning, particularly in literacy and numeracy, take sufficient account of the individual learning targets of individual pupils?**

During the period before identification finally takes place, it is very useful to have some type of system in place for identifying pupils about whom there is some concern and who may be moved onto School Action at a later date. The Record of Concern (ROC) on page 32 may serve such a purpose. It is a kind of pre-record identification that should be used in periods of uncertainty.

Examples of when to use Records of Concern

The following examples serve to illustrate situations when pupils become a cause for concern. Many of these pupils will never need School Action.

Take the case of pupils struggling in Nursery or Reception classes. Teachers often observe that some pupils, on their initial entry into the school, display problems of immaturity affecting their learning or behaviour, which disappear after the benefit of a few months in school. It would not be appropriate to record such pupils as having a special educational need. Nor would it be appropriate to intervene on behalf of a new pupil who enters the school with apparent difficulties; they may, after a period of settling down, begin to cope well.

Problems may occur when a child is undergoing some personal trauma at home – such as parental break-up – which has a temporary effect on the pupil. To misquote what it says on the pill packet, only if symptoms persist should the child be officially registered.

Another possible situation is that a new teacher who takes over a class at the beginning of the year may be tempted to identify several pupils as having a special educational need because of their low level of attainment in literacy, numeracy or both. It must be borne in mind that some classes have become the victims of unfortunate previous circumstances. Their teachers may have been away from school on long-term sick leave, so that they have experienced a series of supply teachers. They may be struggling as a result of poor or inadequate teaching. It is amazing how certain groups of pupils, once in the hands of a competent and reliable teacher, can suddenly take off and lose their potential to be considered as a child with special educational needs. So the message to class

---

Record of Concern

To be completed by the class teacher	Name of pupil _Hannah Williams_
	Class _3_ Age _7yrs 6mths_
	Date of birth _5.8.93_
	Teacher's name _Miss Robinson_
	Today's date _____

Concerns (Please tick appropriate box)   Evidence

Cognition and Learning Difficulties
General learning difficulties ☑ _Hannah's reading age and general literacy skills are well behind peer group_

Specific learning difficulties ☐

Behavioural, Emotional and Social Difficulties ☑ _Hannah has very limited concentration skills. She often strays 'off task' and interferes with the work of other children. She is often disruptive in class._

Communication and Interaction Difficulties
Speech and language difficulties ☑ _Hannah's speech is indistinct. There are certain sounds she has difficulty in saying._

Autistic spectrum disorders ☐

Sensory and Physical Difficulties
Hearing difficulties ☐

Visual impairment ☐

Physical and medical difficulties ☐

NB These categories of special need are as defined in the draft revised Code of Practice, in the section on SEN Thresholds Guidance

How to survive and succeed as a SENCo in the primary school   © LDA 2000

teachers is, be vigilant. The ROC may serve a useful purpose in the interim period. Many pupils whose names go on it will never need to receive School Action.

The ROC has another use. It may be used as the focus of an INSET session (see Section Four, session two) early in the school year to help teachers understand the process involved and avoid premature or delayed identification. A sample ROC is available for your use, (Section 3).

Decisions, decisions

Teachers are often lacking in confidence about exactly what constitutes a special educational need, and when a child should move onto School Action. Perhaps this is why some pupils are either identified too early or very late in the day – not through negligence, but through confusion. It is difficult to lay down specific criteria, but page 46, paragraph 5.13 of the Code suggests that the following information should be utilised:

- **Their performance monitored by the teacher as part of ongoing observation and assessment.**
- **The outcomes from baseline assessments.**
- **Their progress against the objectives specified in the National Literacy and Numeracy Frameworks for teaching.**
- **Their performance against the level descriptions within the National Curriculum at the end of the key stage.**
- **Standardised screening or assessment tools.**

The ultimate indicator for the class teacher, however, must be comparing the achievement, progress and behaviour of the pupil causing concern with that of the rest of the class. If the difference is significant, then clearly this is a case when the pupil should be identified for school intervention. The matter should be discussed with the SENCo, and a mutual decision should be made to put the special needs process into action; then intervention through **School Action** should begin. The Code indicates the following possible triggers for **School Action** (paragraph 5.44, page 52):

- **Makes little or no progress even when teaching approaches are targeted, particularly in a child's identified areas of weakness.**
- **Shows signs of difficulty in developing literacy or numeracy skills which result in poor attainment in some curriculum areas.**
- **Presents persistent emotional or behavioural difficulties which are not ameliorated by the behaviour management techniques usually employed by the school.**
- **Has sensory or physical problems and continues to make little or no progress despite the provision of specialist equipment.**
- **Has communication and/or interaction difficulties and continues to make little or no progress despite the provision of a differentiated curriculum.**

Once the decision has been made, the SENCo should take the lead in acquiring all relevant information in order to complete assessments, plan for the future support of the child and monitor and review the action the school has decided to take. Strategies and targets to assist the child should be recorded on an IEP, for which the class teacher will be responsible. In some cases it may also be advisable to contact outside professionals for advice on an informal basis.

Parents must be informed of this decision, and the most sensitive way is to invite them into the school to discuss the progress of their child. The role of the parent is important in the SEN process and begins with the parent being informed of the school decision to initiate **School Action**. The possible impact of this must be considered, and it is a matter that must be handled with extreme sensitivity. Informing the parent is the first step in achieving parental support and the way this is carried out is important. Issuing a written invitation to come into school to discuss the matter sets the process in motion.

Invitations to parents/carers

The examples of letters on pages 33 and 34 (Section 3), may be copied onto the official school notepaper and blank copies may be given to class teachers to keep in their class SEN ring binders (see Section Two). It is the responsibility of the teacher to send the appropriate letter to parents and provide the SENCo with a copy of the letter to prove that parents have been told of the decision to undertake **School Action**.

Type one (page 33)

This is the initial letter to be sent to parent/carers. It invites them to attend a progress meeting, at which they will be informed. The informing is far less likely to cause upset when the advantages of the situation are explained to them in person. It is important to emphasise that identification is a positive procedure that will ultimately be of benefit to their child.

Type two (page 34)

If the parent/carer does not respond to the first letter, a further letter should be sent informing them about the **School Action** and what the process implies. This time, the parent is given the responsibility to arrange to meet the teacher.

The full co-operation of parents is important for the smooth running of the process. Failure of parents to co-operate may result in the whole SEN process being delayed, and may adversely affect the pupil. If a child does not feel supported by their parent, the incentive to achieve the targets may be affected.

The decision has been taken, the parent has been informed – so what happens now?

The Individual Education Plan

The SENCo and the class teacher must decide, as a result of careful scrutiny of all the information that has been collected, just what the most appropriate **School Action** should be. An IEP should be drawn up, in consultation with the child.

The Code provides the following information regarding the IEP (paragraph 5.50, page 54). The IEP should contain:

○ **the short-term targets set for the child;**
○ **the teaching strategies to be used;**
○ **the provision to be put in place;**
○ **the outcome of the action to be taken;**
○ **when the plan is to be reviewed;**
○ **success and/or exit criteria.**

The IEP should only record targets that are additional to or different from the differentiated curriculum which is already in place for all children.

The targets should be:

○ **crisply expressed;**
○ **no more than three or four in number;**
○ **related to the key areas of communication, literacy, numeracy, behaviour and social skills;**
○ **reviewed termly whenever possible.**

The Code suggests that ideally IEPs should be reviewed termly and further that one of the reviews each year could coincide with a routine parents' evening. This would depend on the wishes of the parent and the anticipated complexity of the review. Reviews should be of an informal nature, and the views of the parent and child should be considered. Whenever possible, the child should be involved in the review process and in setting further targets. The 'My targets' sheet (page 36 of Section Three) is a useful way of involving pupils in deciding on their targets and the 'My week' sheet (page 37) is a useful way for pupils to monitor their own progress towards their targets.

'My targets'

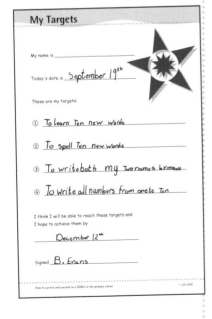

The 'My targets' sheet has been devised because many pupils seem to have no idea what the targets on their IEPs actually are. Clearly, there would be a much greater incentive for them to achieve the targets if they knew what they were. There are also LSAs who support specific special needs pupils yet have never seen the IEPs or been invited to attend review meetings. It is very important that all those concerned with the pupil feel involved and know just what is expected of them.

The 'My targets' sheet may act as a useful form of communication between the LSA (if one is involved) and the pupil as it can be examined regularly, with the pupil ticking the targets on the sheet as they are achieved. This activity keeps the targets clearly in view and helps to keep the pupil on task.

After the IEP has been devised, the teacher should help the pupil fill in the sheet by translating the language of the targets into words the pupil can understand. For example, 'to learn the first 10 high frequency words from the National Literacy Strategy' could be written down by the pupil as 'to learn 10 new words'. The sheet should then be kept by the teacher in the class SEN ring binder, (see page 28), and the pupil and LSA should also have copies.

The 'My Targets' sheet can also be used as a kind of contract between the pupil and class teacher or LSA. It can be examined at regular intervals to monitor progress. If the pupil seems a million miles away from achieving the targets, it is a useful way of drawing attention to lack of progress and then discussing the reasons. Sometimes it is because of pupil absence, sometimes because of a lack of effort on the part of the pupil, and sometimes it is the responsibility of the school – the allocation of insufficient time and resources may have made the achievement of the targets impossible.

'My week'

The 'My week' sheet has been devised because many schools are under so much pressure that there is little time for pupils to stop and reflect. Giving an opportunity for quiet contemplation may help pupils realise that in fact things are not going as they should and that they need to change some aspect of their approach or attitude to work or relationships to achieve more success in school.

This sheet may be used as an activity for all the class, but it is particularly useful for pupils with special needs. However, it is helpful for everyone to stop and reflect on what is going on – even teachers. The sheet may also be used for home/school liaison purposes, to allow the parents to read and understand the child's personal viewpoint, but it should be left to the child's discretion to take it home. It may be that the parents would criticise it or that what the child writes is personal to them and they do not wish to disclose it to anyone.

Children should also be given the opportunity to share the contents of their sheet by teachers inviting them to read out what they have written to the rest of the class, should they wish. This can be a very useful activity as it gives pupils a chance to listen and learn from others about their reflections. This activity may lead to pupils developing a greater insight into themselves. What appears to be a simple activity may actually be a profound one.

Clarification of roles

The decision has been made, the child identified. At this point it will be useful to clarify exactly who does what and when, once a pupil has been identified as requiring **School Action**. It is very important for all those involved with the provision for special needs to be aware of the implications and responsibilities of their role. The SENCo cannot stand alone. As SENCo your first task may be to ensure that all members of staff are fully aware of the SEN policy of the school and of just what is expected from them. In this section we shall seek to clarify the roles of the class teacher, the SENCo, the parent and the pupils themselves. The key question is: Who does what, why and when?

Who is
responsible for
what: School
Action

Who is responsible for what: School Action

The class teacher

The class teacher has the following role:

- ○ Is responsible for the initial identification of a pupil's special needs through observation of classroom practice and on-going assessment.
- ○ Must inform the SENCo of their concern and decide, with the SENCo, if the school needs to help the pupil through the introduction of School Action.
- ○ Should supply the SENCo with all the information necessary in order to assist them in devising an effective IEP for the pupil, which will be in addition to an already differentiated curriculum.
- ○ Must send out a letter to invite the parents to a meeting with the SENCo and the teacher, to discuss the concerns and inform the parents of the school action.
- ○ Decides on the best way for the parents to contribute to the child's achieving the targets on the IEP.
- ○ Arranges and attends any subsequent review meetings with the SENCo, parent and, if appropriate, the child, until such time as the school decides that the pupil no longer requires School Action or that the pupil needs to move on to gain support from School Action Plus.
- ○ Informs the SENCo of any problems that may arise between reviews.
- ○ Organises the timetable, class grouping and all available resources so that the pupil receives all possible support to reach the targets.
- ○ Reads through the agreed targets on the IEP and requests that the pupil fill in a 'My targets' sheet which will act as an informal contract between teacher and pupil.
- ○ Maintains on-going liaison with the pupil regarding progress.

The SENCo

The SENCo's role is as follows:

- ○ Must advise the class teacher regarding the decision to intervene on the pupil's behalf through School Action.
- ○ Makes an informal assessment of the child's needs, if possible, as well as collecting all available assessment and information already held by the school regarding the pupil.
- ○ Provides the class teacher with an SEN ring binder for the purpose of keeping together all information on the SEN pupils in that class and other essential SEN information.

○ Fills in the official SEN paperwork, but distributes to the class teacher any relevant paperwork provided by the LEA which may be more appropriate for them to complete.

○ Ensures that the class teacher informs the parents of the decision by letter, should they fail to respond to the initial invitation to meet the teacher and SENCo, and receives a copy for the pupil's wallet.

○ Organises a colour-coded wallet in which to keep all the information regarding the SEN pupil.

○ Devises the IEP in close co-operation with the class teacher, using the results of the informal assessment or other test results, along with information provided by the class teacher.

○ Informs the parent of the LEA parent partnership services, which should ensure that the parent has access to information, advice and guidance relating to the educational needs of their child.

○ Sends a copy of the IEP to the parent if they fail to attend the meeting.

○ Ensures that there are adequate resources within the school to meet the needs of all pupils who are experiencing difficulties.

○ Arranges and attends the review meetings and advises the parent how they may help at home.

○ Suggests possible resources that could be used in support of the child.

○ Provides the parent with a summary of the school's special needs policy (if available) or shows them the school prospectus, which should include a summary of the SEN policy.

○ Arranges (if at all possible within the budget limits of the school) for the child to receive some support from an LSA.

○ Contacts outside agencies for informal advice and further information if needed.

○ Provides on-going monitoring to ensure the child is making progress by making occasional class visits and examining the teacher's SEN ring binder, where the pupil's progress should have been regularly updated by the class teacher on the assessment sheets.

○ Makes the decision, after a reasonable period of time and in agreement with the class teacher and parent, that the pupil no longer requires School Action or that the pupil needs to proceed on to School Action Plus.

The parent

The role of the parent is important in the SEN process and begins when the parent is informed of the school decision that the child would benefit from the support of School Action. The possible impact of this must be considered, and it is a matter that must be handled with extreme sensitivity.

Some parents experience distress when they hear of the school decision. Parents may not wish their child to be picked out as somehow being different from other pupils. An unfortunate outcome of School Action may be that disappointed parents begin to treat their own children differently, feeling that they are not as good as other children. Most parents, of course, once the initial concern has diminished and they understand that the identification of their child as having a 'special educational need' will mean that the school will take steps to address the need, are pleased that the school has taken action.

At other times, parents themselves may initiate the process. They may feel upset if the school fails to accept that their child has a special need and is not willing to make the extra provision that identification implies.

To identify a child as having a special educational need is an important decision, and the implications of this decision for the child's relationship with the parents, and the parents' attitude to the school, may be more far reaching than the school realises.

The full co-operation of parents is important for the smooth running of the process. Failure to achieve it may result in the whole SEN process being delayed, and also adversely affect the pupil. If a child does not feel supported by their parents, the incentive to achieve the targets may be affected. This is when the support of the teacher may be all important and may, to some degree, compensate for possible lack of interest and support from home.

The parent has the following role:

- **Provides the class teacher and the SENCo with any information which may be relevant, including details about their child's health, early development and behaviour at home.**
- **Participates in their child's effort to meet their targets.**
- **Gives consent for the school to make a request to put the child onto the next phase of support, should this be needed.**
- **Signs and returns copies of any home/school liaison arrangements.**
- **Co-operates with any arrangements made with out-of-school professionals.**
- **Offers support and encouragement to the child.**
- **Supervises the child at home when doing any work which will help the child achieve the set targets, as agreed at the review meetings.**
- **Informs the class teacher or SENCo about any problems that may occur between meetings.**
- **Attends all the review meetings.**
- **Ensures their child is adequately nourished and clothed, acquires adequate sleep and rest and is fully equipped for school.**

You Are A Marvel

... We should say to each of them: Do you know what you are? You are a marvel. You are unique. In all the years that have passed, there has never been another child like you. Your legs, your arms, your clever fingers, the way you move.

You may become a Shakespeare, a Michelangelo, a Beethoven. You have the capacity for anything. Yes, you are a marvel.

Pablo Casals

Who is responsible for what: School Action Plus

The pupil

Now for the role of the SEN pupil, not a minor consideration in the process. The Code says that 'All children should be involved in making decisions right from the start' and 'Practitioners should ensure that the child is involved in the development of the Individual Education Plan and in setting targets.' This is where the 'My targets' sheet may have a valuable role.

First of all, we must view the pupil's special needs as a challenge rather than a problem, so that they will feel encouraged and supported. We know in our own personal lives that our most effective helpers don't take over, but simply show us the way. It is the same with SEN pupils. The school, class teacher, SENCo and maybe the parent and LSA will do their bit, but they need to know the child's answer to the question, 'What are *you* going to do?'

The pupil's role is as follows:

- **Is shown the targets and, before they are set in stone, is asked, 'These are your targets, but what do you think? Do you think these are achievable? Are there any you would like to change?'**
- **Is invited to attend the reviews – or part of the review, if this is advisable.**
- **Completes a 'My targets' sheet recording the IEP targets – the sheet will act as a contract between teacher and pupil.**
- **Is told the outcome of review meetings, even when the parent does not attend.**

(Again, this must be part of the subtle process of encouraging the pupil to take responsibility for their own destiny. The way to do it is to say, 'We are so pleased with you, Dale. You have achieved all the targets!' Or, 'We felt disappointed that you did not achieve all the targets. It may be that they were just too difficult. What do you think? What stopped you? Could it be that you have had too much time away from school? We don't want to set impossible targets for you again.')

The pupil should also:

- **Be given a weekly opportunity to reflect on the work over the last week by completing a 'My week' sheet.**
- **Be aware, through regular informal contact with the teacher, that there is ongoing interest and encouragement regarding their progress towards the achievement of the targets.**

Who is responsible for what: School Action Plus

So much for the roles and responsibilities for **School Action**, when most pupils' difficulties will be addressed. If, after a prolonged period of time (the length is left to the discretion of the school), the pupil is not making the anticipated progress, the school may need to consider moving the child on to the next phase, **School Action Plus**.

The Code identifies triggers for **School Action Plus** as follows (paragraph 5.56, page 55). The pupil:

- **continues to make little or no progress in specific areas over a long period of time;**
- **continues to work at National Curriculum levels substantially below those expected of children of a similar age;**
- **continues to have difficulty developing literacy and numeracy skills;**
- **has emotional and behavioural difficulties which substantially and regularly interfere with their own learning or that of the class group, despite having an individualised behaviour management programme;**
- **has sensory or physical needs and requires additional specialist equipment or regular advice or visits by a specialist service;**
- **has ongoing communication or interaction difficulties that impede the development of social relationships and cause substantial barriers to learning.**

School Action Plus is the time when schools call in the aid of external agencies. The external services should advise teachers about IEPs, strategies and resources that are available for the child. They may act in an advisory capacity, they may provide an assessment, or it may be that teaching support will be available from outside professionals, then the permission of the parents must be sought. It is mandatory for all LEAs to employ educational psychologists and education welfare officers, and there should also be a range of other outside agencies that may be called upon to support the school with further advice or assessments. Typical of the range available are:

- behaviour support service,
- learning support service (for pupils with mild to moderate learning difficulties),
- hearing impaired service,
- visual impaired service,
- pre-school service,
- hospital teaching service,
- speech and language therapists,
- clinical psychologists,
- child psychiatrists,
- paediatric occupational therapists,
- paediatricians.

In addition, there may be other personnel from the health authority and the social services department who could be called upon to provide advice and support. The SENCo should also be aware of and have information regarding voluntary organisations such as bereavement counselling or Gingerbread groups that offer support to single parents.

Roles and responsibilities: School Action Plus

When a pupil has been identified as needing the support offered by **School Action Plus**, further additional responsibilities are involved.

The class teacher

The role is as follows:

- ◗ **Continues to support the pupil in the same way as for School Action, incorporating any possible extra help and resources as specified by the IEPs on behalf of the pupil, attending reviews and taking account of the advice of the outside agency involved.**

The SENCo

The SENCo has the following role:

- ◗ **Informs the school and parents of the decision to initiate School Action Plus on behalf of the pupil.**
- ◗ **Fills in the relevant paperwork for the LEA, who will decide if School Action Plus is appropriate.**
- ◗ **Works in close co-operation with the outside agency selected to provide advice and support for the pupil, class teacher and parent.**
- ◗ **Devises the IEPs in co-operation with the outside agency, class teacher and parent.**
- ◗ **Organises and co-ordinates the review meetings.**
- ◗ **Seeks advice from the literacy and numeracy co-ordinators.**
- ◗ **Completes all the relevant paperwork.**

The roles of the parent and pupil continue as for **School Action**.

Roles and responsibilities: statutory assessment

For a very small minority of pupils, progress through **School Action Plus** may not provide adequate or appropriate support. The Code makes provision for this situation in paragraph 5.62, page 56. After consultation with the parents, class teacher and outside agency, the school needs to make a request for a statutory assessment. Parents also have the right to request an assessment at this stage. Alternatively, the request may come from social services or other agencies who have had close contact with the child. During the period when the LEA is giving consideration to the request, the pupil should continue to be supported through **School Action Plus**.

The Local Education Authority

The LEA need to consider if there is enough convincing evidence. They must decide, within six weeks, if they are willing to carry out a statutory assessment. Should the request for assessment be refused, the parents have the right to take the matter to an SEN tribunal, provided the school made the request or it was requested under section 328 or 329, (see Code, page 89, paragraph 7.71). If a statement is issued, the time from the request for a statutory assessment to the issue of the statement should be no more than 26 weeks.

The head teacher

The head teacher, before referring the pupil for statutory assessment, should ensure the school is able to provide written evidence about:

- the school's action through School Action and School Action Plus;
- IEPs for the pupil;
- records of regular reviews and their outcomes;
- the pupil's health including the child's medical history where relevant;
- National Curriculum levels;
- attainment in literacy and numeracy;
- educational and other assessments, for example from an advisory specialist or an educational psychologist;
- views of the parent and the pupil;
- involvement of other professionals;
- any involvement by the social services or education welfare service.

(See Code, page 56, paragraph 5.64.)

The class teacher

The class teacher will proceed as for **School Action Plus** while the LEA are in the process of making the decision.

The SENCo

The SENCo at this stage:

- Collates all previous information regarding the progress of the child.
- Sends this information to the LEA, with the appropriate paperwork, requesting a statutory assessment.
- Continues to monitor and review the pupil's progress with the class teacher and outside agency.

Once the decision has been made to issue a pupil with a statement some additional responsibilities are required. However, if the LEA decides against a statement, parents and school will be contacted and reasons given for the LEA's decision not to issue a statement.

Roles and
responsibilities:
pupils with
statements

Roles and responsibilities: pupils with statements

The class teacher

The class teacher's responsibility is:

○ **To follow the procedure for the school-based provision, supervising the pupil's timetable to accommodate the hours allocated to the pupil from an LSA.**

The SENCo

The role of the SENCo is to:

○ **Follow the same procedures as identified for the school-based stages, but in addition to ensuring regular IEPs are prepared and review meetings take place, must also submit written reports regarding the pupil's progress for the annual review meetings specified by the LEA.**

○ **Ensure that review meetings are held within the time specified by the LEA.**

○ **Request, on behalf of the head teacher, prior to the date of the review, written advice from the child's parents and any other person who has some involvement with the child.**

○ **Circulate, two weeks before the meeting, copies of all the written advice received, to all parties invited to the annual review.**

○ **Monitor the progress of the pupil (making use of the SEN ring binder) and support class teachers and LSAs with advice and resource suggestions.**

○ **Request that all LSAs fill in monitoring sheets in order to record the progress of the pupils towards their IEP targets (see Section Three).**

○ **Ensure that the LSA is provided with adequate training and information to carry out their role effectively.**

The learning support assistant

It is important that the LSA keeps records on a daily basis of the work carried out with the child. The monitoring sheets may be used as a focus by the LSA, when required to write a report on the pupil's progress for annual review meetings.

Section Two
Managing the special needs provision

The serenity prayer

Grant me the serenity
To accept the things I cannot change
The courage to change the things I can
And the wisdom to know the difference.

This section suggests ways of setting up efficient systems in order to manage, monitor and co-ordinate the special needs provision within the school. This is what you will need:

- ⊙ A four-drawer filing cabinet.
- ⊙ Ring binders – one for every teacher in the school.
- ⊙ Manila wallets – three different colours.
- ⊙ Wall calendar showing all the days of the school year.

The filing cabinet

The filing cabinet

The filing cabinet must lock, as it will contain the pupils' records and paperwork, which are confidential.

It should have four drawers, so that all the essential documentation and resources necessary for the SENCo role can be kept together in one place.

It should be in an area that will provide easy access for the SENCo (not in the head teacher's office, for example) and preferably in an area specially designated for the sole use of the SENCo. Resources for use with special needs pupils throughout the school may also be stored in this area. The ideal would be for this area to be suitable for the SENCo to hold the many meetings that are an essential aspect of the role.

The top drawer

The top drawer will contain:

- ⊙ completed ROCs for pupils who are causing concern,
- ⊙ a complete list of the names of pupils identified as having special educational needs within the school,
- ⊙ the pupils' SEN wallets.

The Records of Concern

These are the records for pupils who are receiving careful scrutiny from the class teacher, but whose needs do not warrant their receiving the support of School Action. These records should be kept by teachers in their class SEN ring binders, but copies should also be kept by the SENCo in a separate folder in the front of the filing cabinet.

The SEN records

SEN records should not be simply a vague list of names arranged under 'School Action', 'School Action Plus' and so on. Comprehensive records should be kept, providing information with reference to the pupils' previous SEN history. This will give class teachers a complete picture of their pupils' backgrounds and will also be a reminder to the SENCo of what progress the pupils are making over a set period of time.

The records set out in Section Three may be photocopied and used. A complete copy should be kept in the filing cabinet, and a back-up copy could be kept on the computer. There are useful software resources available which provide this facility. The records must be updated regularly. Copies of them should also be placed in the teachers' SEN ring binders; these should refer only to the pupils in that teacher's class. The class teachers will be responsible for updating their class SEN records, and must inform the SENCo of any changes. The SENCo is in charge of the school SEN records.

The pupil's SEN wallets

The top drawer should also contain the pupil's SEN wallets. These should be colour coded, according to where pupils are placed, and arranged accordingly. For example:

- ⊙ School Action – green wallets
- ⊙ School Action Plus – red wallets
- ⊙ Pupils with statements – blue wallets

They should be filed in class order for ease of access. If and when it is necessary to transfer a pupil to another stage and consequently a different-coloured wallet, simply stick a white label over the pupil's name so that the wallet may be used again (and again).

These wallets will contain the following:

 All necessary LEA paperwork

Official paperwork varies from authority to authority, but will include sheets for devising IEPs and forms for reviewing targets, which are completed by the SENCo following review meetings. It is very important that the SENCo is familiar with the LEA paperwork and the procedures and expectations regarding the SEN process within their particular LEA. Failure to understand this may result in a delay in addressing the needs of pupils. All LEAs have devised their own policy regarding special needs and all SENCos will need to be acquainted with the appropriate policy.

Assessment information

It is desirable for pupils to have some kind of informal assessment carried out by the SENCo to inform the IEP for **School Action**. This will give the SENCo an opportunity to get to know the pupil, so that they are not just a name on a folder in a filing cabinet. These assessment results will provide a starting point on which to base the IEP targets. In addition, the class teacher's and SENCo's knowledge of what resources, techniques and strategies may be used with the pupil are very important. There will be additional assessments carried out for **School Action Plus** and, of course, for pupils with statements the folder will contain a copy of the statutory assessment.

Current and preceding IEPs

The final IEP is, of course, drawn up in co-operation with the class teacher, but a combination of using assessment results, the class teacher's knowledge and views plus the expertise of the SENCo is likely to produce a sound IEP. For **School Action Plus**, the contributions of the external agency are most important, and the parents should always be included in any consultations.

Any other relevant paperwork

The pupil may have an involvement with an outside professional such as a speech and language therapist and there should be information regarding this involvement. The pupil may have a medical condition; further information here is important.

Photocopies of any letters and invitations sent out to parents by the LEA or professionals regarding this particular pupil

All these should more or less fill your top drawer. You may even have to take over some of the second drawer – but avoid this if you can, as this should be devoted to other important documents. So, what are they?

The second drawer

This drawer should contain all the documents that are useful, or essential, for the smooth running of the SENCo role. SENCos will discover their own favourite documents, articles and books. As a starting point, the following are recommended:

The Special Educational Needs Code of Practice 2002

This sets out principles, practices and procedures that schools must bear in mind when organising provision within the school. All schools and LEAs need to demonstrate that they are fulfilling their statutory duty to have regard for the code.

DFE leaflet 'How can I tell if a child may be dyslexic?'
This leaflet was produced to help teachers identify pupils who may be dyslexic. It provides a series of possible pointers.

The school's special needs policy
All schools must have a policy, which ideally involves all teaching and non-teaching staff. The full policy document must be accessible to teachers, governors, parents, support staff and outside agencies working in the school.

It is a good idea to produce a summary of the policy for parents who may find the full policy somewhat daunting and difficult to comprehend. All parents must also be informed by the governors in their annual report about the special needs provision.

Special Educational Needs: A guide for parents and carers
This guide may be obtained from the DfES and given to parents to explain the whole SEN process. Copies are available from the DfES publications centre, phone number 0845 602260.

The LEA SEN policy
This will indicate to the SENCo the expectations and particular procedures followed by the LEA; it is important that the SENCo takes account of these. Failure to do so may result in a delay in the support offered to a child.

The school's prospectus
This should contain a summary of special needs provision.

Any other relevant materials
There are times when SENCos will need to check certain facts, to deliver INSET to teachers, and to upgrade their own knowledge and skills. Relevant documents should be on hand when such occasions arise. It is useful, for example, to have information regarding medical conditions that are likely to be encountered in school. Some of the materials may simply be useful articles cut from educational journals and magazines.

The third drawer

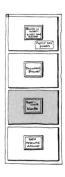

This drawer will contain master copies and prepared photocopied letters and pro formas which are needed on a regular basis. Explanations of these are to be found in Section Three. They are in the following categories:

- ROCs,
- letters to parents (two types),
- letters to professionals,
- LSA monitoring sheets,
- 'My targets',

- ⊙ 'My week',
- ⊙ all LEA blank paperwork.

The SENCo must make sure that supplies are kept topped up. Master copies should be kept together in a ring binder.

The bottom drawer

The drawer will contain photocopies of resources to be used with the pupils that will support them in reaching the targets set on their IEP. These resources should be only for the use of pupils with special needs. It is important that they are clearly labelled and that supplies are regularly replenished. The resources are likely to include:

- ⊙ worksheets to develop fine motor skills and handwriting,
- ⊙ phonic worksheets,
- ⊙ worksheets to support the development of writing skills,
- ⊙ worksheets to assist with reading and cloze procedure,
- ⊙ flash cards,
- ⊙ spelling resources,
- ⊙ numeracy worksheets for pupils with difficulties,
- ⊙ worksheets which are part of second chance reading schemes.

This drawer is to be used only for worksheets. All the other resources for the use of the special needs department should be stored together on a shelf (or hopefully, shelves) allocated, carefully categorised and labelled, with a signing-out book for teachers to use when resources are borrowed. It is important to keep an inventory of all SEN resources and to make sure new resources are added to it.

So much for the filing cabinet.

The ring binders

This is your next type of essential equipment. Every teacher in the school should be provided with a ring binder in which to store all the paperwork regarding special needs provision which is pertinent to them, and in particular to the needs of the pupils in their own classes. The ring binders should include the information set out below, but you may wish to provide particular teachers with additional material relating to the needs of specific pupils. For example, a teacher may need to support a pupil with Attention Deficit Hyperactivity Disorder (ADHD); it is clearly important that they are provided with as much information as possible regarding this condition.

The ring binder for every teacher should contain:

The school SEN policy
By including this you make sure that every teacher, including any supply

teacher who may take over the class for short periods of time, has immediate access to a copy of the policy.

Blanks of letters to parents

These should be of two types. It is the task of the class teacher to inform a parent that their child has been identified as having a special educational need and is to be provided with an IEP. It is important that some kind of record be kept to confirm this. A type one letter should be sent and a copy given to the SENCo for the pupil's SEN wallet. If the type one letter is ignored, then the teacher must send out the type two letter (see Section Three).

ROCs (blanks and completed forms)

The teacher should give copies of the completed ROCs to the SENCo to keep in the folder which the SENCo keeps in the filing cabinet. This gives the SENCo some idea of the potential problems. The teacher's copy in the SEN ring binder will act as a reminder to the teacher to observe the pupil until a decision is made about whether to provide **School Action**.

Relevant assessment information

This is useful as it will remind the class teacher of the information on which the pupil's IEP is based. It should be regularly updated to show what progress is being made.

Current IEPs

It is of course important that the class teacher is aware of all the targets on the IEP so these can be incorporated into weekly planning.

Current class SEN records

There should be a list recording the names and stages of every pupil in the class who has been identified as having SEN. In addition, there should be three separate lists, one for each phase, to identify the action taken by the school, with space to record review dates. Examples are to be found in Section Three. The class teacher will be able to see at a glance when the review meetings are due. Supply teachers will be immediately aware of which pupils have special educational needs. The class teacher must take responsibility for updating the information in the folders.

The SEN ring binder should always be left in an accessible place so that if a supply teacher takes over the class they have all the necessary information. The ring binder, however, contains confidential information, so it should be available only to teaching staff.

The SEN ring binders are very useful in helping the SENCo to monitor what is going on in the classroom. They can be collected in by the SENCo in order to check that the assessment information and the records are all being kept up to date, and that review meetings are arranged and taking place. The fact that

The manila wallets

The wall calendar

teachers are aware that the SENCo checks up regularly on this information means that teachers are much more likely to give it their frequent attention. The SENCo can use the teacher's information to update their own records. It is important that the class information matches the SENCo's central records.

The manila wallets

These are the third type of essential equipment. They are kept in the filing cabinet and are the responsibility of the SENCo, (see page 25).

The wall calendar

This is the fourth, and final, piece of essential equipment. It helps to co-ordinate the whole system. It provides an overview of all the review meetings that should be taking place. If the wall calendar does not show meetings for all the pupils with special educational needs, then the SENCo immediately becomes aware of this fact. They can check with the teacher if this is an oversight or if there is some other reason why the pupil's review meeting is not being held. All pupils with special educational needs should have a review meeting indicated on the wall calendar at least once a term.

Useful
photocopiable
resources

Section Three
Useful photocopiable resources to support the special needs provision

The resources detailed in this section may be used to support the special needs provision in the school. They have all been referred to in earlier sections. The resources are:

- ⊙ ROCs,
- ⊙ letters to parents,
- ⊙ 'My targets' and 'My week',
- ⊙ special needs records pro formas,
- ⊙ record of work to be carried out with special needs pupils (monitoring sheets for LSAs).

Record of Concern

To be completed by the class teacher

Name of pupil _____

Class _____ Age _____

Date of birth _____

Teacher's name _____

Today's date _____

Concerns (Please tick appropriate box)

Evidence

Cognition and Learning Difficulties

General learning difficulties ☐

Specific learning difficulties ☐

Behavioural, Emotional and Social Difficulties ☐

Communication and Interaction Difficulties

Speech and language difficulties ☐

Autistic spectrum disorders ☐

Sensory and Physical Difficulties

Hearing difficulties ☐

Visual impairment ☐

Physical and medical difficulties ☐

NB These areas of special need are as defined in the revised Code of Practice, in the section on SEN Threshold Guidance.

Letter to parents – type one

Dear

I am writing to ask you to call into school in order to discuss the progress of your child _____.

Please could you come into school on:

Date: _____ Time _____

Place: _____

If this is not convenient, please will you contact me to arrange another appointment.

Many thanks
Yours sincerely

Class teacher

Please fill in the reply slip, and return it to the school as soon as possible.

I/we will/will not be able to attend the meeting regarding the progress of my/our child.

In Class _____ on _____

Signed_____ (Parent/guardian)

Letter to parents – type two

Dear

I am sorry you were not able to attend the meeting to discuss the progress of your child _____ .

In view of the difficulties your child is currently experiencing in school, it has been decided to take School Action. This means that the school will offer extra support for your child, and progress will be carefully monitored. It would be very helpful if we could discuss the matter further, and I would be pleased if you could contact the school to arrange a meeting. In the meantime, I enclose a copy of the Individual Education Plan containing targets that we hope _____ will achieve by _____ , when the review meeting is to be held. I also enclose a summary of the school's special needs policy to provide you with further information.

Yours sincerely

Class teacher

'My targets'
and
'My week'

'My targets' and 'My week'

These two sheets are for the use of pupils. Their use is explained on pages 14 and 15. On this page there are completed examples of each.

My Targets

My name is _____

Today's date is September 19th

These are my targets:

① To learn Ten new words

② To spell Ten new words

③ To write both my Two names by myself

④ To write all numbers from one to Ten

I think I will be able to reach these targets and I hope to achieve them by

December 12th

Signed B. Evans

How to survive and succeed as a SENCo in the primary school

My Week

Name Beth Evans

Date friday october 12th

The best thing that happened to me this week was

I won second prize in the Art competishion

The worst thing that happened to me this week was

I dropped my tray in the dinner cantene

The best work I did this week was

I wrote a story about zarka from mars

The work I could have done better this week was

My multiplicathions

Next week I will try harder with

listening to the teacher

Signed B. Evans

How to survive and succeed as a SENCo in the primary school   © LDA 2000

My Targets

My name is _____

Today's date is _____

These are my targets:

① _____

② _____

③ _____

④ _____

I think I will be able to reach these targets and
I hope to achieve them by

_____

Signed _____

My Week

Name _____

Date _____

The best thing that happened to me this week was

The worst thing that happened to me this week was

The best work I did this week was

The work I could have done better this week was

Next week I will try harder with

Signed _____

Special needs records pro forma

Special Needs Records   School Action   Year Group _____

Name and date of birth	Parents informed: date	Initial meeting: date	First review: date	Second review: date	Outcome

Special needs records pro forma

Special Needs Records School Action Plus **Year Group** _____

Name and date of birth	Outside agency involved	Initial meeting: date	First review: date	Second review: date	Outcome

Special needs records pro forma

Special Needs Records Pupils with Statements **Year Group** _____

Name and date of birth	Date of statement	Provision specified in the statement	Date of review

Record of work to be carried out with special needs pupils

To be completed by learning support assistants

Date	Activity	Observations	Staff

Pupil's name   Class

Section Four
Ideas and resources for in-service training

The Code of Practice indicates that an important part of the role of the SENCo is to provide training for all the staff – teachers and LSAs – to ensure their competent delivery of the SEN provision. To some degree parents require training as well, though this does not concern us here, for the training concerned is that needed to enable parents to help their children reach the targets on their IEPs; such training would take place at meetings when the IEPs were reviewed.

There are five main areas regarding the provision of special needs that SENCos need to convey to staff. This section of the book is devoted to offering guidelines and resources to ensure effective delivery. Many SENCos feel very anxious in their role of INSET provider, but the first time is always the worst. You will be able to deliver the goods with minimal anxiety if you use the advice in this section.

There are occasions when an outside professional should be invited into the school to give the staff the benefit of their particular SEN expertise. The SENCo can't know everything! This kind of visit is particularly important when the school has a pupil with particular difficulties – a pupil who has been diagnosed with autism, for example. All the staff (including the lunchtime supervisors) must be given the training to deal with these particular children.

Here are guidelines and resources for five suggested sessions, to help you with your delivery.

Let's start with a warning. Make sure that everything is ready. There is nothing worse than everyone arriving while you are trying to locate the overhead projector, or you can't find enough chairs to go round or when you have forgotten to photocopy essential materials. I speak from bitter experience. When things get off to a bad start, they never seem to get better. All the resources you will need for the sessions which are provided for you in this section are indicated with an asterisk. Some of the sheets, as you will see, are meant to be used as overhead transparencies. You will need to prepare those in advance of the meeting.

Here are your suggested sessions. You may have a need to cover additional areas; that depends on the circumstances in which you find yourself. The sessions are under the following headings:

Session one: the SEN policy
Session two: the identification of pupils with SEN
Session three: clarification of the special needs roles: who does what
Session four: target setting for pupils with learning difficulties
Session five: SEN resources for pupils with learning difficulties

Session one

Title:	the SEN policy
Time:	approximately one hour
Venue:	the staff room
Intended audience:	all members of staff and the SEN governor
Resources:	Every member of staff to bring with them their own copy of the school SEN policy. The SENCo will also need a copy of the policy.
Programme:	Decide which sections of the policy are suitable for whole staff discussion. Read through these sections with the staff, with brief discussion after each.

The purpose of this session is two-fold. First of all it ensures that all staff are familiar with the contents of the SEN policy. The policy must:

⊙ outline basic information about the school's special educational provision;

⊙ provide information about the school's policy for the identification and assessment of and provision for pupils with SEN;

⊙ provide information about the school's staffing policies and partnerships beyond school.

Secondly, the policy should be reviewed annually anyway, and involve staff in discussions to explore just how effective the policy is in terms of the progress and attainment of pupils with special needs in the school. It is essential that the views of the staff are sought on this matter, and that they have a say in what may need to change. For example, the staff may feel that the way pupils are initially identified needs to be examined, or they may feel that parts of the policy are confusing and should be expressed in a clearer fashion. However, the governing body and the head teacher are actually responsible for developing and reviewing the policy, and any suggested changes must meet with the approval of the governors. It is a good idea to invite the SEN governor to these meetings concerning the policy (all schools must have a named governor responsible for special needs). If, as a result of the meeting, you decide any minor changes need to be made, then the SEN governor should take the ideas to the governing body to gain their approval.

The policy must continue to meet the requirements of the Code of Practice.

Close: Review the session and decide on any change that is appropriate.

> Well, it didn't go too badly.
> Next time, I'll change the starting time,
> some people found it hard to get here.

Session two

Title: the identification of pupils with SEN

Time: approximately one hour

Venue: the staff room (or wherever will comfortably take the OHP, screen and staff)

Intended audience: All teaching staff, including LSAs who are involved with special needs pupils. It may be expedient to invite the school governor who has responsibility for special needs.

Resources: Overhead projector and screen
  *One blank ROC for each person (see page 32)
  *OHT 1 – the special needs process: a graduated response
  *OHTs 2–5 – areas of special educational need
  *OHT 6 – a completed ROC

Programme: This session will equip teachers with the knowledge they need to identify which pupils will require School Action, and which should be acknowledged merely as a possible cause for concern. It will also remind them of the areas identified in the Code of Practice and help them to be vigilant in identifying a need.

1. Discuss the model recommended in the Code of Practice. Use OHT 1.
2. Discuss each area of SEN as defined in the Code of Practice. Use OHTs 2–5. Involve the staff. Discuss when a child's difficulty becomes a problem, which would involve school taking **School Action**.
3. Provide every member of staff with a blank ROC (Section 3, page 32) and invite them to fill in each area. They need to focus on the type of evidence they would require before deciding to place a pupil at **School Action**. It is a good idea to carry out this activity in pairs to promote discussion.
4. Show your completed ROC (OHT 6).
5. Go through your evidence for every area and invite comments and questions from the staff.
6. Ask the staff to think about specific pupils in their own class and decide which area or areas best describes their special needs.
7. Plenary session including question time.

Close: That went well.
I think everyone has more ideas now.
The screen isn't very good – wonder if there is any cash for a new one?
Be glad to get home tonight.

The special needs process: a graduated response of action and intervention

School Action: the SENCo will take responsibility for gathering information and co-ordinating the child's special educational provision, working with the child's teachers, literacy and numeracy co-ordinators, the parents and the child.

School Action Plus: teachers and SENCo are supported by specialists from outside the school.

Statutory assessment: the LEA considers the need for a statutory assessment and, if appropriate, make a multi-disciplinary assessment.

Statemented provision: the LEA consider the results of the statutory assessment and, if appropriate, make a statement of special educational needs and arrange, monitor and review provision.

Areas of special educational need (1)

*Taken from the draft Code of Practice (July 2000).

Cognition and learning

A. General learning difficulties

* Low levels of attainment across the board in all forms of assessment, including, for young children, baseline assessments.

* Difficulty in acquiring skills (notably literacy and numeracy) on which much other learning in school depends.

* Difficulty in dealing with abstract ideas and generalising from experience.

* A range of associated difficulties, notably in speech and language (particularly for younger children) and in social and emotional development.

B. Specific learning difficulties

* Difficulties with fine or gross motor skills.

* Low attainment in one or more curriculum areas, particularly when this can be traced to difficulties in some aspects of underlying literacy and/or numeracy skills.

* Indications that the low attainment is not global; these might include: higher attainments in other curriculum areas which do not make demands on the areas of weakness; higher performance measures of reasoning or ability which do not make demands on the area of weakness; higher attainments in one mode of recording or presentation than in another (for instance better oral than written work).

* Signs of frustration and low self-esteem, in some cases taking the form of behaviour difficulties.

* Evident difficulties in tasks involving specific abilities such as sequencing, organisation or phonological or short-term abilities.

* In younger children particularly, language difficulties such as limited skills in verbal exchanges or in following instructions.

* Evident difficulties or delays in forming concepts, especially when information requires first-hand sensory experiences.

Areas of special educational need (2)

Behavioural, emotional and social difficulties

* Age-inappropriate behaviour or behaviour that seems socially inappropriate or strange.

* Behaviour which interferes with the learning of the pupil or their peers (e.g. persistent calling out in class, refusal to work, and persistent annoyance of peers).

* Signs of emotional turbulence (e.g. unusual tearfulness, withdrawal from social situations).

* Difficulties in forming and maintaining positive relationships (e.g. isolation from peers, aggressiveness to peers and adults).

Communication and interaction difficulties

A.   Speech and language difficulties

These may be identified in the following ways:

* Problems with the production of speech.

* Difficulty in finding words and putting them together in meaningful and expressive language.

* Problems in communicating through speech and other forms of language.

* Difficulties and delays in understanding or responding to the verbal cues of others.

* Difficulties with the acquisition and expression of thoughts and ideas.

* Difficulty in understanding and using appropriate social language.

* Frustrations and anxieties resulting from a failure to communicate, possibly leading to apparent behavioural difficulties and deteriorating social and peer relationships.

Areas of special educational need (3)

Communication and interaction difficulties (continued)

B. Autistic spectrum disorders

These are characterised by a triad of impairments in social relationships, social communication and imaginative thought. Look out for the following:

* Difficulties in attuning to social situations and responding to normal environmental cues.

* Evidence of emerging personal agendas which are increasingly not amenable to adult intervention.

* A tendency to withdraw from social situations and an increasing passivity and absence of initiative.

* Repressed, reduced or inappropriate interactions, extending to highly egocentric behaviour with an absence of awareness of the needs or emotions of others.

* Impaired use of language, either expressive or receptive; this may include odd intonation, literal interpretations and idiosyncratic phrases and may extend to more bizarre expressive forms and limited expression, reducing the potential for two-way communication.

* Limitations in expressive or creative peer activities, extending to obsessive or repetitive activities.

Sensory and physical difficulties

A. Hearing impairment

* Changes in certain areas of academic performance, such as deterioration in handwriting or other areas of academic performance, tonal changes in speech, progressive failure to respond to verbal cues or increasing requests for the repetition of instructions.

* Physical changes such as persistent discharge from the ears, tilting of the head to maximise verbal input, excessive efforts to focus on the teacher's face when instructions are being relayed.

* Signs of frustration with themselves or others, leading to emotional or behavioural problems not previously observed and for which there are no obvious causes.

Areas of special educational need (4)

Sensory and physical difficulties (continued)

B. Visual impairment

* Deterioration in certain areas of academic performance; these might include deteriorating handwriting, slowness in copying from the board, increasingly asking for written instructions to be given verbally.

* Deterioration in other areas such as hand–eye co-ordination, excessive straining of the eyes to read the board, needing to be at the front of the group to look at television programmes or share in story/picture books.

* Progressive anxiety and tentativeness in certain physical activities and an associated reticence in moving around the playground, suggesting that mobility is becoming impaired.

* Evidence of associated stress leading to withdrawn or frustrated behaviour.

C. Physical and medical difficulties

Some children who experience physical and medical difficulties have no problems in accessing the curriculum and learning effectively. In these cases there is no evidence to suggest they have a special educational need.

Those pupils who have physical needs already identified or a medical diagnosis will need to be carefully monitored for their educational needs by school.

Attention should be paid to the following:

* Evidence of difficulties in the other areas of special educational need as set out in the draft Code of Practice (July 2000).

* Impact of the physical or medical difficulty on the pupil's confidence, self-esteem, emotional stability or relationship with peers.

* Impact of the physical or medical difficulty on classroom performance (e.g. through drowsiness, lack of concentration, lack of motivation).

* Impact of the physical or medical difficulty on participation in curriculum activities.

OHT 6   Record of Concern

To be completed by the class teacher

Name of pupil **Sally Jones.**

Class **Y3.**   Age **8 years 1 month.**

Date of birth _____

Teacher's name _____

Today's date _____

Example of one type of evidence teachers may notice, and which would need to be monitored carefully, before deciding if the child has a special educational need.

Pupils would usually only be identified in one category, but at times, there may be evidence of need in additional areas.

Concerns   (Please tick appropriate box)   Evidence

Cognition and Learning Difficulties

General learning difficulties   ☑
Low reading age / knows $\frac{45}{120}$ high frequency words / limited phonics knowledge.

Specific learning difficulties   ☑
Discrepancy between oral and written skills / low self-esteem / very good at science.

Behavioural, Emotional and Social Difficulties   ☑
Finds it hard to stay on task / agressive to peers and adults / refuses to work / no friends / won't accept praise.

Communication and Interaction Difficulties

Speech and language difficulties   ☑
Has poor comprehension / unable to follow instructions / limited expressive vocabulary.

Autistic spectrum disorders   ☑
Poor communication skills / unable to work in a group / very withdrawn / unable to stay in seat /

Sensory and Physical Difficulties

Hearing difficulties   ☑
Talks loudly / does not follow instructions - copies other children / easily frustrated and upset.

Visual impairment   ☑
Poor handwriting / strains eyes to see the board / holds book close to eyes.

Physical and medical difficulties   ☑
Appears tired and listless / eyes glaze over at times / very withdrawn / no enthusiasm.

NB These categories of special need are as defined in the draft revised Code of Practice, in the section on SEN Thresholds Guidance.

Session three

Title: clarification of the special needs roles: who does what

Time: approximately one hour

Venue: a comfortable room which will hold the OHP and screen and which everyone will fit in

Intended audience: the staff and if possible the SEN governor

Resources: Flipchart or black/white board
Overhead projector and screen

*OHTs 7–8   the role of the class teacher: School Action
*OHT 9   the role of the class teacher: School Action Plus
*OHT 10   the role of the SENCo: School Action
*OHT 11   the role of the SENCo: School Action Plus
*OHT 12   the role of the parent
*OHT 13   the role and needs of the pupil
*OHT 14   the role of the governing body

Programme:

1. Begin by discussing the process, as identified in the Code, through which pupils are identified as having special educational needs.
2. Invite class teachers to discuss what they see as their role regarding responsibility for special needs. Ask them all to divide into twos or threes, ensuring that non-qualified teachers and new members of staff are with more experienced members.
3. Write up their comments on a flipchart (should you be so lucky as to possess one) or the board.
4. Discuss OHTs 7 and 8.
5. Back to groups to discuss what they think the SENCo does.
6. Write up comments on the flipchart or the board.
7. Show OHTs 10 and 11.
8. Invite general discussion regarding the role of the parent. Show OHT 12.
9. Repeat for the pupil. Show OHT 13.
10. Show OHT 14. Briefly go through the role of the governing body.

Close: Review what happened.

Hope the car isn't still making that peculiar noise.
If it is must drop into the garage on my way home.
Hope it's nothing expensive.

The role of the class teacher: School Action (1)

Makes initial identification of pupil with special needs and, in consultation with the SENCo and parents offers the child support with School Action (SENCo prepares wallet for filing cabinet).

Arranges a meeting with parents to discuss the school decision to initiate School Action. Explains to parents that the curriculum will continue to be appropriately differentiated to meet the needs of their child, but in addition the pupil will benefit from having their own IEP, with specific targets to suit their needs.

Sends out letter to inform parents of decision to offer School Action, if the parents fail to respond to the initial invitation to a meeting. Gives a copy of this letter to SENCo for the pupil's wallet and sends a copy of the IEP to the parents.

Helps to devise IEP with SENCo, parents and pupils.

Ensures that the IEP targets receive sufficient teaching time and resources for the pupil to be able to achieve them.

Arranges dates of reviews and fills them in on the SENCo wall calendar. Sends out review invitation to parents.

The role of the class teacher: School Action (2)

Differentiates the curriculum in all subject areas, when appropriate.

Monitors the progress of pupils and regularly updates any assessments in SEN ring binder.

Informs the SENCo of any problems that may arise between reviews.

Attends reviews, whenever possible. Provides SENCo with report if unable to attend.

Liaises informally with parents regarding their child's progress towards the targets.

Maintains ongoing liaison with the pupil regarding progress; uses the 'My targets' sheet, signed by the pupil, as a form of contract.

The role of the class teacher: School Action Plus

Continues to support the pupil as in previous stages.

If the pupil is provided with the support of an LSA, must provide a timetable. The LSA should be involved in the planning and liaise with the teacher.

Record sheets must be kept by the LSA, of any work carried out with the pupil and copies of these sheets should be placed in teacher's SEN ring binder.

Should attend review meetings and take account of advice of outside professionals, and how this may impact on all areas of the curriculum, for the benefit of the pupils.

The role of the class teacher: Pupils with statements

When a pupil receives a statement, the procedure is similar to that for School Action Plus. The class teacher must also prepare a written report to present at the pupil's annual review meeting, and help the LSA with the preparation of their report for the meeting.

The role of the SENCo: School Action

Conducts in-house, informal assessment, specifically devised to investigate the needs of pupil with learning difficulties.

Gathers additional information from class teacher, through discussion, test results and any other appropriate sources, and fills in relevant LEA paperwork.

Sets up IEP with class teacher, parents and pupil using the information from the assessment to inform the IEP.

Attends initial meeting to discuss with parents the decision to initiate School Action, and describes ways in which the parent may help their child at home. Provides parents with a copy of the IEP and the DfES SEN Code for parents and carers.

Discusses IEP with pupil; asks pupil to complete a 'My targets' sheet (or the class teacher may perform this task).

Monitors the pupil's progress by checking the teacher's SEN ring binder and observing the teacher's updating of record sheets. Further monitors progress at review meetings, when the IEP will be reviewed and new targets set (use updated assessment for target-setting information). The decision to remove the pupil from School Action or put them forward for School Action Plus will also be made at a review meeting.

The role of the SENCo: School Action Plus

Meets the appropriate professional and devises an Individual Education Plan for the pupil based on their recommendations and also in co-operation with the class teacher and parent. Arranges subsequent review meetings.

Decides, in agreement with the parent, teacher, outside agency, head teacher and governing body, if (following a period of being supported by School Action Plus) a pupil requires a statutory assessment. If so, it is usually the responsibility of the SENCo to fill in the paperwork, collect the evidence and apply to the LEA for a decision.

The role of the SENCo: pupils with statements

On behalf of the head teacher, ensures that all relevant people are invited to the pupil's annual review meeting and that all those involved prepare a written report in the time specified.

Ensures that a suitable room is available for the meeting and that the parents, in particular, are made to feel welcome in what can be a difficult situation for them.

Following the review meeting, sends back to the LEA the completed report, recommendations and paperwork in the specified time, proposing new targets for the pupil for the year, if appropriate.

The role of the parent

Agrees to help their child at home with specified IEP targets when appropriate.

Offers support and encouragement to their child; ensures that the child attends school regularly; supports the child with any homework that may have been set; ensures that the child wears glasses if appropriate, or is equipped with other resources necessary for progress in school.

Attends the review meetings.

Informs the class teacher of any problems that may occur between the review meetings.

Co-operates with any arrangements made with out-of-school professionals.

Provides the class teacher and SENCo with all relevant information about issues that may be impeding the progress of the child.

Takes care of the child's physical needs: sufficient sleep, diet, clothing, regular health checks (if appropriate) and so on.

The role and needs of the pupil

Must be involved with deciding targets on IEP and sign the 'My targets' sheet.

Should receive feedback after each review meeting, or attend if appropriate.

Should be encouraged to see the IEP as a positive procedure.

Should be offered all possible support to achieve the targets, through differentiation of the curriculum and the provision of appropriate resources and teaching strategies to cater for individual needs.

May have to accept some responsibility if the IEP targets are not achieved.

Has the benefit of extra teaching support from an LSA, when available. It may also be appropriate to involve other pupils, e.g. paired reading, precision teaching.

The role of the governing body

Ensure that provision is made for pupils with special educational needs.

Make sure that a responsible person – the head teacher or a named governor – is told by the LEA when a child has special educational needs and that those needs are made known to all who are likely to teach that child.

Ensure that teachers are aware of the importance of identifying and providing for children with special educational needs.

Consult with the LEA and others, when that is in the interests of co-ordinated special educational provision in the area as a whole.

Report each year to parents about the school's policy for children with special educational needs.

Ensure that parents are notified of a decision by the school that SEN provision is being made for their child.

Ensure that children with special educational needs are allowed to join in all school activities whenever that is practical and compatible with the efficient education of other children in the school and the efficient use of resources.

Have regard to the Code of Practice when carrying out their duties towards all pupils with special educational needs.

Session four

Title: target setting for pupils with learning difficulties (literacy)

Time: approximately one hour

Venue: the staff room

Intended audience: all teaching staff, LSA, SEN governor

Resources: Flipchart or board
Overhead projector and screen
    *OHT 15– summary of assessment on Della Scott

Photocopies of blank IEPs of the type used in school – one for everyone

Programme:
1. Show OHT 15. Discuss the findings.
2. Ask the staff to decide in pairs what the four priorities are that will form the targets on the IEP.
3. Feedback from staff. Write the four agreed priorities on the board.
4. Discuss.
5. Now ask staff to devise an IEP based on the four areas of priority. Use the format of IEP with which the staff are already familiar. Emphasise that the targets they set should be achievable within 12 weeks (the time when the review meeting is due) and that the targets should be SMART – Specific/Measurable/Achievable/Realistic/Time targeted.
7. Compare and discuss.

This INSET is directly related to session five, since it is important to relate targets to resources available in school. Ask the teachers to keep their partially completed IEPs, or gather them in and keep them yourself until next time.

Close: Review the session.

> I must spend some extra time with the NQT.
> This was all new to her and I could see that she found it difficult.
> Must do the shopping on my way home.
> Must get milk, don't want to endure another cup of milkless tea.
> Then the paper shop to pay the overdue paper bill.

Areas of difficulty   Della Scott. KS2. Year 4.

Sight Vocabulary

Comment   Knows $\frac{50}{112}$ high frequency words (NLS)

Phonics

Comment   Knows all initial sounds, but confuses b/d.
Unable to cvc blend consistently.

Spelling

Comment   Can spell $\frac{30}{112}$ high frequency words

Independent writing

Comment   Is able to write a short story, but does
not use any punctuation - no full stops or capital letters

Fine motor skills/handwriting

Comment   Della's writing is neat All letters
are correctly formed

Sequencing

Comment   Della was able to sequence 6 pictures
correctly, and tell the story

Class reading book

Title of book   Oxford Reading Tree Stage 5.

Read at ~~accurate~~/frustration level?   But inappropriate*

Any other difficulty noticed?

Della's maths not an area of concern.
Has low self-esteem. Contributes little to class
discussions. Few friends Needs a lot of re-assurance.
*Della said this is a 'baby' book.

Session five

Title: SEN resources for pupils with learning difficulties (literacy)

Time: approximately one hour

Venue: the area where all the SEN resources are stored (if there is such a place); if not, take the resources to the meeting and show them to the staff in the usual venue

Intended audience: all teaching staff, including LSAs who work with SEN pupils and SEN governor

Resources: These will depend entirely on what the school has. It is a good idea to store and label resources to help staff select appropriate ones. The resources you have should cover areas such as these:

- **Developing a basic sight vocabulary**
  Worksheets
  Flash cards
  Games
  Precision teaching materials
  A second-chance reading scheme
  ICT resources

- **Phonics**
  Tapes
  Worksheets
  Precision teaching sheets
  Games

You will also require a selection of resources to support pupils with the development of fine motor skills, sequencing, comprehension, expressive vocabulary, maths, grammar and writing.

Programme:
1. Indicate where the resources are stored and the purpose of each one.
2. Allow the staff to browse through what is there.
3. Emphasise the importance of recording in the notebook supplied which resources they have borrowed, and of ensuring they are returned as soon as possible.

Close: Review the session.

Must get some extra resources for the development of fine motor skills.
Didn't realise how little we had, and this appears to be causing problems in lots of classes.
How much longer to the summer holidays?

Conclusion

Conclusion

I hope that you feel you have profited by reading this book. It may be that all you have gained is reassurance that you are doing all you can in your school and are covering most of the issues raised. If so, be reassured.

You may, on the other hand, decide that some of the ideas and resources provided here would be useful to you. If you decide to reorganise your whole provision, I hope you find that makes a difference. And do remember, Rome wasn't built in a day.

OFSTED

OFSTED

This book would not be complete without reference to OFSTED! Remember, the whole school is expected to share responsibility for SEN pupils. Your job is to co-ordinate it.

The inspectors will certainly want answers to the following questions:

- Are staff aware of their responsibilities? Are they carrying them out?
- Are statutory requirements being met? (Inspectors will certainly check on pupils with statements. All statements will be scrutinised if there are 5 or fewer, and 50 per cent of them will be checked if there are more than 5.)
- Are the funding issues satisfactory? How much money is allocated and how is it spent?
- Are the needs of all pupils with SEN being met? Do all those who require them have IEPs and are their targets being addressed?
- Have issues relating to SEN that were mentioned in the last report been implemented?
- Are resources, including the human ones, well managed?
- Is external support available and well used in the school?
- How well is the progress of pupils with SEN monitored and evaluated?
- Have the LSAs received training? Are they being monitored?
- Has the school taken steps to meet the requirements of the 2002 Code of Practice?

If you have an inspection pending, and feel that you would like to reorganise things, prepare an action plan so the inspector knows that you are aware of, and have plans to deal with aspects of the SEN provision which need attention.

Final thought

Final thought

The human beings who matter most in all of this are the children. They are the ones who will suffer ultimately if we don't get it right. This is why it is so important to make sure you are doing the very best you can. You can make a difference.